Written by
Rox Siles

Illustrated by
Alice Pieroni

Published in association with Bear With Us Productions

This book is dedicated to my son **Alejandro who** fills my
life with joy and makes Christmas truly special.

I thank **my family** and **friends** for all of their support.

There were just a few days left until Christmas Day. Santa knew that **the best day of the year** was just around the corner.

Each day, the mail carrier elves
sorted through thousands of letters
arriving from children all over the world.

"Santa, please bring me a **doll**," said Sallie. She speaks English.

"Papá Noel, me gustaría tener un robot, por favor,"
"Santa, I would like to have a robot, please,"
said Miguel. He speaks Spanish.

"Père Noël, je voudrais une trottinette, s'il vous plait,"

"Santa, I would like a scooter, please,"

said Jacques. He speaks French.

The creative elves kept busy at the toy shop.

They **loved** making toys for all the girls and boys.

The reindeer spent time **training**
for their **Christmas Eve flight**.
They lifted weights and ran on the treadmill.

Christmas Day was getting closer.

"Santa, did you check the list **twice**?"
asked Jackson the elf.

"Don't worry, Jackson!
I still have a few days.
I'm busy ice fishing right now,"
said Santa.

The next day, Mrs. Claus asked,

"Santa, do you know who has been **naughty or nice** this year?"

"I'll get to it tomorrow, Mrs. Claus.
I'm busy building a snowman,"
Santa replied.

"Santa, did you try on your
suit to see **if it fits**?"
whispered Valerie the elf.

"Don't worry, Valerie!"
said Santa.
"It should fit just right.
I'm busy making snow
angels right now."

Christmas Eve soon arrived.
"I will go **sledding** before I travel all
over the world,"
thought Santa.

"Yippee!"
Santa sledded down from the tallest hills again and again.

RIIIIIIINGGGG!

"It's showtime!"
the elves yelled with excitement.

"Oh no!" shouted Santa.
He was running late.

Santa hurried home and put on
his red suit, but it was too tight!
Santa jumped in the sleigh,
but he could barely fit in.

Some of the toys fell out as the sleigh took off.

Sallie **got coal** even though her name had been on the nice list.

Sallie began to cry.

Miguel got a robot, but it only spoke French. Miguel spoke Spanish and couldn't understand it.

He felt very confused.

Jacques got a doll,
but he wanted
a scooter.

"What happened?"
he questioned.

Santa had forgotten to check his list twice!

Santa barely made it to the last few houses on time.

He slid down the chimney too fast and **knocked over** the cookies and milk.

The reindeer didn't have time to eat their magic food and started to run out of energy.

They dragged Santa's sleigh slowly through the sky.

"Ahhhhhhh!"

Finally, the last child on the list
saw Santa by the Christmas tree.

Santa got **startled** when
the boy caught him.
They both began to scream!

"Ahhhhhhhh!"

Santa slowly opened his eyes
and looked into his magic snow globe.

"It was all just a bad dream!"
he thought.

He saw that all the children were happy playing with their toys.

Santa also saw his elves and reindeer **dancing** at the North Pole.

Santa and Mrs. Claus joined them by singing carols and celebrating a **Very Merry Christmas.**

Merry Christmas
God Jul!
Vrolijk Kerstfeest!
Feliz Navidad!
Katá Christouyenna!
Joyeux Noël!
Sheng Dan Kuai Le!
Frohe Weihnachten!
Šubh krisamas!
Buon Natale!
Feliz Natal!

The End.

About the author

Rox Siles was born in Bolivia and moved at a young age to the United States. She grew up in Michigan where she got married and attended medical school. She currently works as a physician in Ohio.

This author developed a passion for writing children's books after reading bedtime stories with her son. One night, they couldn't agree on which book to read. It was at that moment they created "Charlie the Turtle and the Muddy Birthday Cake," and the rest is history.

On her free time, Rox enjoys spending time with her family and their two dogs, Tika and Jazz, which you may find in some of her books.

Her stories are often influenced by their family adventures and her Spanish heritage. Rox's goal is to share positive messages with children through her bilingual books.

CPSIA information can be obtained
at www.ICGtesting.com
Printed in the USA
BVHW021542200721
612420BV00007B/962